cu00706868

# ACKNOWLEDGEMENTS

With great respect and adoration I want to thank the all mighty all powerful God for the opportunity to compile this booklet for his glory through Christ Jesus.

Also a big thank you to my family and friends who have believed in the gifting of God on my life.A special thank you to a dear friend Evangelist / prophetess Evelyn Yeboah whose selflessness and support has been amazing.

Also a big I love you to a great and strong woman of God my mother Exilta.

I pray that as you go through this book, you will experience a miracle, and your life will never be the same.

Psalms: 50-15 call upon me in the day of trouble I will deliver thee, and thou shall glorify me.

# FOREWORD

My ministry is to the abuse, the hurting, the hopeless, the unloved, the depressed, those who have basically given up, the motherless, the fatherless, the lonely, the depressed, struggling with habits.

There is hope in Christ Jesus.

This book is written with you in mind.

Jeremiah 33: 3 Call upon me and I will answer thee and show thee great and mighty things which thou knowest not.

# CONTENTS

# Hold on change is coming:

All biblical quotes is taken from KJV and NKJV

# CHAPTER ONE

## THE PROBLEMS OF LIFE.

Matthew 14. 24   But the ship was now in the mist of the sea tossed with waves for the winds were contrary.

A you going through a storm?

You will meet up with storms in life. The disciples of Jesus faced the storms themselves. Matthew 14: 23-33.

What is your storm today: is it rejection, lack, sickness, family problems, childlessness, marital issues, unemployment.

**Your story will change.**

## AFTER PRAYING THESE PRAYERS MAY YOUR LIFE NEVER BE THE SAME AGAIN.

- ❖ A you struggling to make it in life
- ❖ Are you stuck in a place and can't move forward
- ❖ Is your marriage under attack
- ❖ Does everything you put your hands to fail
- ❖ Do you feel like a failure
- ❖ Are you an outcast in your home
- ❖ People don't take you seriously
- ❖ One step forward seven steps backward
- ❖ Are you having bad dreams at night
- ❖ Has someone told you that you will never make it and amount to anything
- ❖ Everyone you know seems to be getting married but you
- ❖ Cant find gainful employment
- ❖ Business is failing
- ❖ Rejection in your church
- ❖ Do you feel like you cannot fit in with others
- ❖ Are you going through a divorce
- ❖ Do you feel trapped in your situation
- ❖ Do you feel like you cannot cope with the difficulties life throw at you
- ❖ On the edge of a breakdown

If you fall under one or more of the above category you are sure qualified for Gods grace and mercy. God is going to work out something for you.

I just want you to know that it is not over until God says so.

Whatever the plans of the devil, and the people who avail themselves to work for him or the problems that come with life, concerning your life it shall definitely not stand.

After praying these prayers you will begin to walk a winner. Amen.

Renewed hope and dreams will be yours.

Your life will move from stagnancy to success.

This book is for you, not because I say so but because Jehovah God saw your needs.

Father in the name of your son Jesus Christ of Nazareth, I place this person who is going through any of the troubles stated above in your loving hands. They are tired, they are crying out for help. You have said that your eyes are on the righteous to deliver them. Show your power in the life of this one. Their strength is failing, the pressure is surmounting. I pray at this very moment that you will fill this one with your peace. Change that situation around them, let it be disgraced and put to shame for good. Let your child now rise above this problem father, in Jesus name I pray. Amen.

For those who are going through lack send provision. Joblessness give employment, marital issues bring peace and renewed commitment, habits send deliverance, low self esteem give confidence, abusive relationship send help. Whatever their situation may be this day, father, by the authority that is given me in Christ Jesus, I command every situation to bow and leave their life. And right now let your peace and happiness, abundance and good health replace these issues.

I call forth a great destiny for this one in Jesus name Amen.

# CHAPTER TWO

Before we move on to these prayers, I want to ask you a question

Have you made Jesus the lord of your life?

If the answer is yes you are at a good place. God is already working on your situation to bring solution.

If you have answered no to this question and you truly want God to work on your behalf and answer your prayers, take this opportunity to invite Jesus in your life. He will help you out in your circumstances.

What would it profit a man to gain the whole world and lost his soul? Pain.

Have you ever considered what will happen to you after death?

There are two options, Heaven or Hell. There are no in betweens as we were taught. The bible is clear. Heaven or Hell.

Depending on how you live your life, your spirit will leave your body and go to Heaven or Hell.
That will depend on the decision you make .To get to Heaven you need to accept Jesus in your life

If your answer is yes I want to make Heaven and have God work on my behalf,

This prayer is for you

## Open your mouth and make this declaration.

**Lord Jesus I am asking you right now to come into my heart, I am a sinner, forgives me of every wrong that I have done. I believe you are the Christ the son of God who died on the cross for my sins. From this day take your place in my life and help me to live my life to please you. Amen**

Well done you are on your way to a victorious life through Christ Jesus.

Many Christians walk around with their face buried in the ground prayer less while the enemy is busy plotting their downfall

The heart is deceitful above all things and desperately wicked, who can know it.

There are people who are fighting your life even right now as you are reading this book to bring destruction and confusion. These types of people the bible call them the wicked and evil.

God open the eyes of the prophet and took him spiritually into their temple to see the evil that was being done.

Look, whether your situation is caused by someone who is praying evil prayers over you, or whether it was from your own action. Regardless to which it may be, because you are now serving Jehovah God, I want to let you know that your present situation will not determine your tomorrow, you are coming out. Amen.

The devil is not a nice boy: the bible says he is like a roaring lion walking around seeking whom he may devour. If you avail your self and entertain him he will come in and use you in any way he can, and mess up your life. He doesn't take casualties he takes victim.

He has claimed so many lives, and destroys many to alcohol, drugs, greed, prostitution, gangs and the lot. Some he uses to do witchcraft and all manners of cultism. But it does not have to be you.

Some he uses to backbite and tell all manners
Of lies, which is equally destructive.


## Allow God to raise you up

God has set before you an open door and no one can shut it. Rev 3-8

Trust God today beyond what you can see and feel. God will change your situation quickly.

Your life will become a success story.

Jeremiah 29: 11 For I know the plans that I think towards you. Plan to prosper you and not harm you to give you hope and a future.

I declare over your life today that your future is great. Amen

# CHAPTER THREE

**NOT VERY LONG AGO**

Not very long ago I enter into a wilderness season, everything seem to be going wrong with my life. Opposite to the word God had been speaking for my life. In other words it seems like all of hell had broken loose days became months, and months became years. You see the problem that is design to kill you or to take your peace, Will not, because, the answer simply is: JESUS. JESUS will not allow it. WE are just too precious to him.

Let me encourage someone out there in their wilderness to hold on and DON'T GIVE UP.

I want to share this true story with you. On my evangelistic travel to West Africa. I met up with this lovely lady, who had assigned herself with the church to prepare our meals. She made a promise to herself and God that she would take care of strangers who travelled from a foreign land, by catering for their food, because of the painful experiences she went through on her life journey.

Her story goes like that. By the age of 14 her parents were about to marry her off to a sixty eight year old man who already had three wives living with him. As you can imagine to the dismay of this young girl her only option was to run away or become wife number four. She ran away to another village where she was not known. In that village she befriended a young man about her age group, who would later become her husband. She told him about her predicament, he took her to his mum. There she retold her story, the mum took her in. This young lady was well trained, a good cook, and quiet efficient in the home. She quickly became a favourite with the family. The mum promised her to her son, as an arranged marriage.

They were both sent to continue on their education, the son to London and the girl to America. They both did medicine and later became doctors. The young man joined her in America and there they began their married life and career. The husband became a medical doctor, she worked her way up also functioning as a qualified medical doctor. Life seems promising.

Now about 20 years later they receive a telephone call that her mother in law has passed on, the husband went home to do the burial. The wife stayed on due to other obligation. After the burial he called his wife to update her. He promise to call her later that evening, but instead she receive a call saying that he was rushed to the hospital, barely fifteen minutes later she got another call that he had passed on. Immediately she and the kids made flying arrangements. On her arrival in Africa she learnt that her husband was already buried, without her consent. The husband went home to burry his mum and the next day after his mum burial he too was buried, without his family being there. That was the beginning of this lady two years of sorrow.

Let me just mention that before this lady travelled her pastor in America warned her that she should not make that travel and that it was a set up. She thought to herself that her pastor is a selfish man to tell her not to travel to Africa to burry her husband. Soon after she arrived she understood the word from God through the man of God. Her sorrow had begun.

Her father in law demanded the wealth of his son from her. She told him she is not aware of the wealth he is talking about. He was not convinced. He continue to demand the wealth of his dead son, he had convinced himself that there was millions. The woman said to her father in law that just in case he knows something about that kind of money that she is not aware of, tell her where the money is kept and she will share it with him. He insisted she had the wealth of his son, and he threaten her in no uncertain term that within four months he would kill her, and that she would never set her feet in America again.

A few days later her bag went missing, with all of her documents and money. Many trips to the American embassy were futile. Her name could not be found on the American system. She submitted her national insurance number but the face of her dead mother in law would show up instead of her face. Her problem had begun. She thought maybe she will get through in a different location, she travelled to another part of Africa, but to no avail. She seems to be fighting a loosing battle, her father in law words was becoming a reality in her life.

Out of desperation, as it was now becoming months and she could not go back home to her job at the hospital and her children in college, she remembered a school friend in the west of Africa, she went to stay with her. After more unsuccessful attempt of getting her documents sorted, the friend tried to get her into prostitution. She told her friend that she apparently did not know her very well, and left. It was during this period of time that she understood the true meaning of hunger. She was practically homeless and penniless.

A friend told her about a man of God and introduced her to the ministry. The ministry embraced and supported her, they stood in the gap in prayer believing God with her, through the rough times. They were a pillar. She called the pastors her life saver. Two years later she is holding her American Passport and travel document. God has proved the devil a liar. She did not die in four months and she had gotten her documents. Now there remained another problem she needed to overcome. Whenever it came to her day of travelling she get so sick, that the airplane refuse to carry her in that condition. As soon as she reaches home she is well. Again weeks became months. On many attempts she couldn't step feet into that aircraft without getting sick.

This is the point of her life where we met during my missionary visit alongside some mighty men and woman of God I was graced to be a part of in West Africa. As this doctor gave herself to doing Gods work by taking care of our meals, in return we gave what we have we blessed her life and pray that she will set her feet back on American soil. She was due to travel the following week of my departure, she again was unable to do so. I called to find out whether she had left, she did not, she miss the flight again, but booked for the following Monday. you see this woman faith will not let her give up and all those around her will not give up as we now has joined in prayer that she will travel and be with her children in America. You see if the devil doesn't give up why should we give up.

What am I saying: I am saying to someone who is going through great troubles, Don't just give up. You shall not die but live to declare Gods word in your life. Like this lady God will do it for you. It's not because this lady is special that God did it, it's because of the mercy of God that is available to all who will call on him.

## Continue to serve God and do what is right.

- ❖ Christ Jesus is your peace in the storm.
- ❖ He will block the plans of the enemy concerning you.
- ❖ He will expose their wickedness.
- ❖ He himself will fight for you.

Stand back and see the salvation of the lord for the Egyptian that you see today you shall see no more.

These problems you are facing will pass: God will turn it around for your good. It will only prepare you and make you a better person. Amen.

There are many people who have walked the road where you are at today and they have made it. We hear of the greatest testimonies of those who lost hope and lost all and with the backing of Christ Jesus and a determined mind they were able to turn their lives around.

May this be your portion. Amen.

It will be well with you. Within each of us, God has put a great strength. Don't ever say you do not have strength, it is in you.

I am now going to pray for the areas of your life that comes daily under attack.

# CHAPTER FOUR

**Jesus said to Satan I have nothing of you. John 14:30**

Therefore any areas in your lives that have given Satan legal access to come in I am going to shut it in Jesus name.

All these little things you do, the things you say, the places you go, how you live, allow Satan access.

Let's shut that door. So the Holy Spirit can begin his work in you.

Pray these prayers.

- ❖ Lord Jesus close the door of access to the evil one in my life.

- ❖ Anything in my life that is hindering me to be successful, flee in Jesus name.

- ❖ Anything in my life that represent sin, let it be removed by fire, be it backbiting, stealing, lying, adultery, fornication, backbiting, homosexuality,

**whatever it may be remove it by your power ooh God.**

❖ **Lord as I do my part do yours**

**Matthew 6:33 seek ye first the kingdom of God and his righteousness and all these things shall be added.**

**May I declare over your life that as you serve God faithfully he will restore you.**
**You will have more than enough, you will get that promotion you are seeking for, that car you are needing it will come, the husband you are looking for you will get, that wife you desire to have you will get. God will add these things to you.**

**Nothing will stop you from receiving all that God has planned concerning you.**

❖ **You will have a testimony.**
❖ **You will have a breakthrough.**
❖ **You will fulfil your dream.**

**You see you have a high priest who has gone through the heavens and is making intersession for you. He had to go pass the principalities and powers, they are all under his feet.**

**Every problem that is over your head is under God's feet. Isn't that great news.**

**Pray this prayer.**

- ❖ This year I will get to my right position.
- ❖ Nothing will stand in my way.
- ❖ I will meet up with the people that really mater.
- ❖ I will meet the right people who will help me to my destiny.

# CHAPTER FIVE

Does it sometimes look like you are not progressing? Everyone around you seems to be doing better, but you are barely holding. Great testimony is coming in around you and you are wondering when will it be your turn. Its not that you are not faithful to God, but nothing seems to give.

This prayer is for you.

God is about to change that for you, testimonies will come. It's just a matter of time.

You will get the victory God will get the testimony.

The greatest testing of ones faith is waiting.

- ❖ In the wait there will be pain.
- ❖ In the wait there is preparation.
- ❖ In the wait is frustration.
- ❖ But there is also victory in the wait.

Abraham the father of faith experienced all. We are no exemption.
How we wait before God is in prayer.

The Psalmist David encouraged us:

Wait on the lord be of good courage and he will strengthen thy heart wait I say on the lord.

It may seem like God is not going to show up in some cases. But this is where we must learn to trust him. It is not about what we think, but it is about what his word says, and God is faithful to his word.

Ecclesiastic 9:11 I returned and saw under the sun that the race is not to the swift, nor the battle to the strong, neither yet bread to the wise, nor yet riches to Men of understanding, nor yet favour to men of skill, but time and change happen to them all.

God is not partial, he does not look at how pretty you are to bless you, or how smart you may be, he does not look at your qualification, neither your ability to bless you.

Even when we don't deserve he blesses us.

We give God thanks for his wisdom here or else lots of us would be surely out of the race.

Let's just take some time there to thank the lord.

Lord I thank you that the race is not just for the swift or the battle for the strong, neither is bread just for the wise, nor is riches only for men of understanding. I wait my time and change. Amen

# CHAPTER SIX

A you seeking God for something

Isaiah 49-18

God is saying to you today that I will answer your prayers because I have a set time when I will help by coming to save you.

Do not give up on yourself.

**GOD HAS A SET DATE FOR YOU**

Father in the mighty name of your son Jesus Christ remembers these ones reading this book. I do believe it's in their hands because you want to do something special for them. Hasten ooh father to help. Amen

Be sober be vigilant, your adversary the devil walks about like a lion seeking whom he may devour.

- ❖ Any evil eyes that have put their eyes on you May God blind these eyes. Amen.

- ❖ Any monitoring spirit that is sent to check on your progress, I send confusion to them in Jesus name

- ❖ I command the fire from heaven to fall on the strong and stubborn enemies

❖ They will not have the last say in your life.


## Cover yourself before you go to bed at night

❖ Use the blood of Jesus
❖ Release mighty Angels
❖ Call the fire of God.

I release the blood of Jesus to protect you, and those under your roof. I call on the mighty angels to surround your home. I call the fire of God to build a hedge around your surroundings. May your body be to hot for them to handle. Amen

## All power belongs to God.

It is no way that you will serve God and keep on suffering.

God will show up for you.

❖ Live a holy life.
❖ Pray.
❖ Stand on Gods word.
❖ God will move you from bondage to dominion, from the pit to the palace.
❖ He did it for Joseph.
❖ Any power holding your destiny captive God will take it down. Amen.

Luke 10:19 Behold I give you power over all the powers of the enemy.

## Strength

**You are not as weak as you think you are, rise up and begin to fight with prayer for your life and the life of your love ones.**

**The power of God in you must supersede that of the enemy that is fighting you.**

**The bible clearly state that we wrestle not against flesh and blood. Ephesians 6**

**God himself will frustrate the plans of the crafty, so that their hands cannot carry out their work.**

**The God of heaven himself is fighting for you**

## Say with me:

**Lord frustrate every plan the enemy throw at me, let everything they try to do to me fail.**

# CHAPTER SEVEN

## DELIVERANCE

**Obadiah 1:17 But upon mount Zion shall be deliverance and there shall be holiness and the house of Jacob shall possess her possession.**

**In my home there shall be deliverance and their shall be holiness and I shall possess my possessions. Amen.**

❖ **I pray deliverance in your home and in your life.**

❖ **The lord shall deliver you from every evil.**

❖ **Every good thing in your life that has been stolen by the enemy, today I take it back by force In Jesus name. Amen**

**And the Lord shall deliver you from every evil. 2Timothy 4:18**

**Meditate on this scripture passage. Keep it in your spirit, believe that word for your life and situation, personalize it into your daily prayer, and pray it like this:**

**And the Lord shall deliver me from every evil.**

The Lord will release mighty angels around you because you have called on God through his word, when the:

Arrow of sickness comes the angels will block it. When the arrow of paralysis comes the angel will block it, when the arrow of madness and frustration comes the angels will block it, when the arrow of lack and bondage is released the angels will block it.

That's the power of prayer through God's word.

Do you know that the wicked pray also, they are even more dedicated and determined in prayer than the child of God. They have their source the devil, whom they chant, and make incantation to.

Their prayer will go that way:

This one will not make it. Before she reaches 30 she will go mad, she will never give birth and if she does, the child will not live. And their list goes on.

We hear the saddest stories of how lives have been destroy through these medium, but it will be minus you in Jesus name. And sadly enough it's mostly someone who knows these people, and who they know that is working such evil acts against them, as I mentioned earlier in chapter 3.

One experience that have remained with me and it has also opened my understanding is that of a woman whom, at first I thought was mentally unwell until listening to what was coming from her mouth.

In the year 2010 I visited my hometown, walking in the town, in and out of shops I happen on a grown woman who at that time I thought was mentally unwell, until I heard what was coming from her mouth. She was walking the street, speaking to herself, at a voice that was audible to passersby, she stopped, turning around, facing the north, she turned around to the east, then the south and then the west in doing so she was chanting and cursing the prime minister . I stood up for a few minutes looking at her in amazement, surprise at the poisonous words of witchcraft coming from her mouth. Immediately I reverse what I had overheard her saying. I asked for God's divine intervention and protection on the gentleman's life.

I am repeating this story to alert you, that the wicked, whether you know them or not it don't matter, they know you; they are looking at your life and some wont rest until they have secured your downfall.

This gentleman has no idea that someone has made it their point of duty to be praying for his downfall. Yes in his Position it is expected, likes and the dislikes. But that level of personal evil mission of chanting and cursing and wishing this kind of evil and madness to his person. I do not think so.

Let's pray.

❖ Anywhere my name is being called for evil, I cancel your assignment. it will not be so

❖ Anyone who is speaking curses over your life, I reverse that curse back to sender let it go back into their belly.

❖ May God cover your head in the day of battle.

❖ The God of Abraham, Isaac and Jacob arise and work on your behalf.

❖ The God who answered Elijah by fire, so also destroy by fire the works of the evil ones towards you.

❖ Every good thing in your life that has been stolen by the enemy today, we are taking you back by force, I take back your job, peace of mind, your finances, your good health, your children, your marriage, your glorious destiny, in Jesus name.

❖ In the name of Jesus, I demand a return of all of your belongings. This battle is the lords, and you shall not loose in Jesus mighty name. For great is God in you.

# CHAPTER EIGHT

## DIVINE PROTECTION

Be strong and of good courage, fear not or be afraid of them, for the lord thy God, it is he that go with thee, he will not fail thee or forsake thee. Deuteronomy 31:6

Keep in mind that there is none that can deliver out of God's hand.

- ❖ May the lord keep your feet and none of your steps slide

- ❖ May the lord keep you from all that you are struggling with today.

- ❖ May God restore your self esteem

- ❖ May God hide your face from your enemies.

- ❖ May God lift you up

- ❖ May God give you a testimony

- ❖ May the voice of rejoicing be heard in your house

- ❖ May God fight those who fight you

- ❖ May you fulfil your destiny

- ❖ May you overcome your enemies{sickness, etc) by fire by force

- ❖ You are highly favoured of God.

- ❖ May you experience God in a fresh way

- ❖ May God see you through every storm

- ❖ May your enemies hear of all the good things that God is doing in your life

If you will just hold on a little longer, you will see the hands of God, and you will laugh again.

## FEAR AND DOUBT

Let's deal with fear and doubt.

Fear can hinder ones destiny. Doubt is a killer of faith Gods word says to cast down every imagination that exalts itself against the knowledge of Christ Jesus

Hold on to God's word closely, read the word of God it's your greatest weapon against the enemy.

Pray

- ❖ You spirit of doubt holding my mind captive leave in Jesus name.

- ❖ You spirit of fear, I reject you from my life. Amen.

- ❖ I refuse to give up because I know Jesus will never let me go.

- ❖ I will keep my eyes on Jesus, and I will believe that God will come through, because I know he will.

- ❖ I will put my faith to work.

- ❖ I will lean not on my own understanding but in all of my ways I will acknowledge Jesus.

# CHAPTER NINE

## Do you know that you can change the mind of God.

In the book of 2 kings 20. When God send the prophet Hezekiah to the king to let him know that he should prepare for death because he was going to die. The king went before God and pleaded for his life, he wanted more time, the bible says that he prayed to God and wept sore before God. In other words he humbled himself. God heard his prayer and immediately God instructed the prophet to go back and tell the king that I have added twelve more years to his life.

What is it that you require from God today?

The quality of your relationship with God can change his mind concerning you. God is always there waiting for us to come to him. When we do wrong things we automatically move away from him.

God don't change. He said, "I am the God that changes not. His ears are always open to our cry.

Jesus is the truth, the source and the answer to all our prayers, every other power must bow.

## WHY IS THE DEVIL BOTHERING YOU

He knows God has great things in store for you. He will do his best to stop you. When you pray and turn your attention to Jesus you defeat him. Keep on doing that.

Some of us have not had a good beginning neither a good middle, but God is giving us a great ending story.

- ❖ You are born to prosper, you will make it.

- ❖ When you are going through life's difficult moments, hold on to the word of God.

- ❖ Remind God of his words concerning you

- ❖ Walk in obedience.

- ❖ Don't just sit and take life's punches, fight back in prayer.

## FOR THOSE GOING THROUGH DELAY

Jesus is the truth the source and the answer to all your prayers.

Every power must bow.

When we pray we take back everything the devil steals from us, and we stop his plans to ruin our lives and to stay on top.

We are going to now pray some dangerous prayers. These prayers may be that which will hold your life together, and open doors of opportunity.

## Don't you dare give up

Pray this prayer aloud, with boldness and authority.

Any power working against my life, my family, my marriage, my finances, my every children, my health, today let go in Jesus name. I bear the mark of Jesus on my body you have no control over my destiny scatter in Jesus name. Galatians 6:17

Any power working on top of my head to press me down and oppress me hear ye the word of the lord drop down and perish in Jesus name.

Any power that is  behind my back that is sent to pull me back and to stop me from going forwarding in  life receive fire and burn to dust in Jesus name.

Any power on my right side to keep me shut in drop and consume to ashes in Jesus name.

Any power operating on my left side to box me in that I cannot move and make progress in life drop and die in Jesus name.

Any power in front of me sent to stop my progress so that I will not be able to go forward, you that foul spirit sent to block, my pathway of reaching the finish line, where all my blessings are, I send blindness, I send confusion, I send the double edged sword of the lord to pierce you asunder, let the fire of God consume you. I release the wind of God to blow your remains away back to hell in Jesus name.

I declare over your life that you have moved from defeat to victory in Jesus name Amen.

## Pray out loud

I declare that I have moved to another dimension.
My destiny is sealed in Christ Jesus
My life is counted worthy from now on
My mind is lined up to the word of God.
I am covered in the blood of Jesus. Amen

Father thank you for taking me to a place where you are the centre of my focus, perfect your will in my life, let every day of my life be a pleasure. You are truly an awesome God. Teach me how to be humble in your presence. I give my life over into your loving hands. Daddy, you are in control.

# CHAPTER TEN

**THIS SECTION IS FOR THOSE WHO HAVE EXPERIENCE PHYSICAL OR SEXUAL ABUSE FROM THE HOME OR SOMEONE THEY KNOW.**

One of the greatest epidemics is the rampant of physical and sexual abuse to the most vulnerable, the children and young people who are helpless to defend themselves. Many will grow up to be dysfunctional hurting people or abusers themselves.

We therefore thank God for the precious blood of Jesus who will restore healing to the minds and heart of those who have suffered at the hands of their abusers, as they seek him.

## DON'T COMPARE JESUS TO YOUR FATHER, HE IS HOLY

To someone out there I want to say it is alright to call Jesus father and acknowledge him as the father you have never hard. You see Jesus is not like men. You can't compare him to your father or any other father figure who has brought you pain. He is God, he is supreme he is holy and has no sin in him. When you call upon him, he will bring peace to your heart and

situation. He is the Lamb of God, he is gentle and kind and compassionate.
Allow him to heal your hurt.


## LET'S PRAY.

FATHER IN HEAVEN, I THANK YOU FOR THE LIFE OF THIS ONE YOUR  DAUGHTER / SON WHO  IS GOING THROUGH SO MUCH HURT AND SHAME BECAUSE OF THE  SHAMEFUL ACT OF THOSE WHO SHOULD  HAVE CARED FOR THEM BUT HAS HURT THEM SO BADLY INSTEAD. LORD MANY OF THEM ARE SO BADLY BROKEN IN SPIRIT THAT THEY FIND IT DIFFICULT TO LOVE AND TRUST OTHERS AGAIN. I ALSO PRAY FOR THAT MOTHER THAT FATHER WHO HAS NOW GROWN UP WITH A FAMILY OF THEIR OWN AND IS FINDING IT DIFFICULT TO COPE. LORD JESUS YOU SAID IN YOUR WORD THAT YOUR MERCY IS ENDLESS AND IT'S NEW EVERY DAY. I ASK THAT YOU BRING COMFORT TO THIS ONE. WRAP YOUR ARMS AROUND THEM OOH LORD. LET THEM FEEL YOUR HOLY PRESENCE AND EXPERIENCE YOUR PEACE IN THEIR SITUATION. BRING COMPLETE HEALING TO THAT HEART. TOUCH THIS AREA IN THEIR HEART THAT ONLY YOU CAN AND LET THESES ONES BEGIN TO FIND JOY AND PLEASURE IN LIFE AGAIN. IN JESUS MIGHTY NAME. AMEN


I believe that if you have prayed this prayer right now God is comforting your heart and healing your spirit.


NOW YOU REPEAT THIS PRAYER.

- ❖ **LORD JESUS I NEED YOUR HELP IN MY LIFE.**
- ❖ **CLEANS AND PURIFY ME FROM THE INSIDE OUT WITH YOUR PRECIOUS BLOOD.**
- ❖ **WASH AWAY EVERY FILTH OF ABUSE FROM MY PAST.**
- ❖ **CLEANSE MY MIND AND MY HEART AND REMOVE ALL TRACES OF LINGERING PAIN.**
- ❖ **LORD RIGHT NOW I RELEASE MY ABUSER AND LEAVE THEM IN YOUR HANDS.**
- ❖ **FORGIVE ME OF ALL OF MY SINS.**
- ❖ **AND BY FAITH I BELIEVE THIS DAY THAT I AM FREE OF THIS BONDAGE IN JESUS NAME I PRAY.**

**Psalm 109: 26-27 Help me, oh lord my God. Oh save me according to your mercy. That they may know, that this is your hand that you lord has done it.**

## A YOU BELIEVEING GOD FOR CHILDREN OF YOUR OWN

There are some married couples who have been trying to get pregnant for years and it has not been happening for you, take courage, this prayer is for you.

The woman with the issue of blood had her condition for 12 years. It sure is a long time to be in that condition. Like you she could have been hoping to have a child, but her situation would not allow her, like you she may have spent all her money trying to get well, her situation did not change until Jesus arrived on the seen.

## MAY JESUS ARRIVE ON YOUR SEEN TODAY.

Father touch the womb of that woman who needs a miracle to conceive. Rearrange every facility inside her reproduction system and let them begin to function well to conceive, in Jesus name amen.

Father touch that man that is believing you for his healing rectify low sperm cells and give him the capability to reproduce in Jesus name we pray amen. Give them children, and let the children be, as olive plants around their table. Amen. Minister to these ones right now father.

# CHAPTER ELEVEN

## Stubborn situations that won't go away.

There are some situations that are just so hard to go away. Does it feel like you have been praying for ages and the problems is getting worst. It is the trick of the enemy. He desire for you to loose faith and quit, therefore he will intensify the pressure. His aim is to get you to give up.

Psalm 37: 3-4   Trust in the Lord and do good so shall though dwell in the land and verily shall thou be fed. Delight thyself also in the Lord and he shall give thee the desire of thine heart.

That's a promise from God. Hold on to it and don't let go. God will not fail you. Everything under the sun has an expiring date and this Problem will expire to. God will work it out for your good.

## A prayer for the body of Christ / the family

I want to speak to these men and women, who have lost their way and have moved from the order of God, but is still in the forefront of church doing the right things in their own eyes and that of men, but is failing miserably in the home and the family circle. You will have to give to God an account for your actions. Wise up, repent. God is still looking for men and women who will serve him in spirit and in truth.

God still want to raise up Generals to do his work as in the bible days. The devil has entered into the churches. He is now ruling from the pulpit to the pew. He entered suttle but he is now ruling openly. Repentance and baptism is a thing of the past in most of the churches.
But we give thanks to God our father for the faithful few in our mists who care about saving souls and helping people to escape hell fire and helping the poor.

Father in the name of your son Jesus Christ, I bring this man/ this woman who is functioning before men but truly their heart is far from your precepts. Father for your name sake I pray that you will open the eyes of their understanding so that they may see the damage that they have done, repent and turn around, so that you Lord will get the glory and the enemy will be defeated.

Satan has infiltrated the church and the family. Men of God have caused such hurt and shame in the pulpit, that many have lost faith and have returned into the world. Greed, power and womanising has become associated to the name of certain men of God, but there is a remnant who has not bowed to Baal.

Remember child of God the devil has his and God to have his, the bible says by their fruits you shall know them. Do not be deceived. But do remember that there are some trustworthy men of God who are after

Gods heart and truly care about the wellbeing of Gods people and are of good report.

Today I want to encourage someone out there who has been a victim of these pastors who misrepresented God, do not loose your soul salvation because of them. God is real, men fail but God cannot fail. Do not focus on men; trust in the one who saved you. If you are not comfortable in a church move out, God is not restricted despise what men may say. Listen to the wisdom of God in you, live true, live holy, God will lift you up.

## GOD WANTS TO USE YOU TO SHOW HIS GLORY.WALK WORTHY.

# CHAPTER TWELVE

## Is there hope

Someone may ask the question I am a prostitute how can I serve God and I am living at the brothel. If God has touch you right now you will have lost your taste and desire to be a part of this lifestyle and all that is happening around you. You are on our way to a different and rewarding lifestyle that will positively affect you and others differently.

You may be reading this book today and you may say I am a Gang member and I have done so much wrong. If you truly want change in your life and you allow God in, he will not judge you for yesterday He will forgive you. But from this moment on you will be accountable. Today is your day to change the circumstances around your life and invite Jesus in.

You can be on your way to a new start
Sign yourself a contract with the lord ask the blood of Jesus to seal this covenant.

Hold on to it in difficult moments believing and knowing in your heart that God has honour this covenant and as you hold on to your side he will do his part.

## MY CONVERSION

When I got converted to the Lord in 1998 I didn't fully understand all that was happening. One thing I understood for sure is that I had lost the desire for many things. A week later I gave up smoking cigarettes, I lost the appetite for partying, gave up a relationship, and all these things I indulged in. my family and friends and those around me didn't really understood what was happening to me at that time.

I remember spending all my spare time at home praying and just enjoying quiet time with the lord. Quite the opposite of this person who never let a good party and disco on a Friday and Saturday night go unattended. My sister got concerned and called my friend to come take me out. She meant well. Neither one of us then really understood what God was doing with me.

You see God knows exactly how to take one out, separate and cleanse that one for his work and purpose.

God has a plan for your life to.

During that time I was working at a casino as a supervisor. Don't ever let anyone tell you that where you are at you cannot serve God. If he save you there in his own time he will move you and open the doors you need to go through. God has timing for everything concerning your life.

People will try to pull you down and discourage you. They may not even understand you. Do not be discouraged. Hold on to God even more so, God has a way of working things out.

People may look at your life and present situation and write you off. Joseph was sold into slavery by his brothers, lied on and labelled a rapist by his master's wife. Made headline news, thrown into prison by Potifar and soon forgotten in the pit. Many years before he was betrayed by his brothers.

In a dream God showed Joseph that his life would be great, but God didn't tell him the difficulties he would encounter before he would achieve that greatness.

Remember God is faithful to his word. When his word came the gift that God had given Joseph made room for him and took him directly into his destiny. Psalm 105:19-20.

Do not give up on hope. Do not give up on you, and do not give up on God. God is watching over his word to bring it to pass concerning you. Like Joseph May your word come that will remove the limit on you and take you before great men.

I ask God right now to set a watchman over your affairs. To protect your destiny and that of your love ones.

# CHAPTER THIRTEEN

A you frustrated at your progress and where you are at in life? Know that you are not alone. Others have walked and are still walking this path. Do not remain in this place of frustration, find something to do that is rewarding, and occupy your time wisely also with prayer as you wait your change.

When a man looses hope he has lost everything. Because he has played himself right in the hands of his adversary the devil. Today you can allow your heart to start hoping again. It's a choice. No situation is permanent. There is a time and season for everything under the sun. Ecclesiastes 3

If you are aware of the burdens that others are facing, right now you will thank the Lord for where you are at , but don't stop there thank him also for what he is about to do for you.
As you trust God with your life he will validate that trust and help you out.
Remember that God do not always work the way you think is best or how you want it to be. In Gods wisdom he will do what is best for you that will give permanent solution, peace and joy to your future. Not a quick fix that most likely will end in disaster later down the road. God is a wise God.

While going through some personal experiences, my eyes were rudely opened to the fragility of marriage, family, and commitment. This also opened my eyes to look at the married families around me and how they are struggling to keep it together. Marriages and family is truly under attack, in the Lord or not in the Lord. You see marriage is of God and the devil will fight that union.

When you look around you what do you see. Much pain, sorrow broken homes, neglected and abused children. Society breaking down, Parents correcting their children by using inappropriate language. That child most likely will grow up and continue that pattern on their children and those they come in contact with unwanted teenage pregnancy, unnecessary killing and fighting. Parents have lost control of their children because they are either not around or too busy to train and nurture them.

If we take time to apply biblical foundations as in proverbs 6: 1-4 our success story will be much higher and better.

I speak to a father our there who has abandon his family, the children don't have to suffer to. God entrusted them in your hands, you need to man up and take responsibility. Be there for your children be a part of their life. What you would have wanted from your own dad, you can give it to your children. Don't make them a statistic. You will have to give God an account for these children and how they turn out.

Boys love to play football game or go fishing with their dad. Appreciate them; it won't cost you anything but your time.

You this mother out there who has done a runner on your family and left your children to pursue drugs or for whatever the reason. A child needs a mum. It's in their makeup. God wants you to be selfless. They did not ask to come into this world, you gave them the gift of life, give them also the gift of a good mum. You will not regret it in your old age.

We admit life is not always easy, the decisions we make are not always the best, but there are ways of coping and restoration. Find a local church, build a network of people who can support you and your family. Everybody needs somebody at one time or another in life. You are no exception.

Your children are the future, doctors, lawyers, president, teachers, and pastors. Pilots. Let's support them. All they ask for is a normal childhood; all they want is a mum and dad who are there for them.
In so doing we a building a healthy society and pleasing Jehovah God.

Like Paul  we will be able to say : I have fought a good fight, I have finish my course, I have kept the faith, henceforth  there is laid up for me a crown of righteousness.


❖ May the Lord meet you at the place where you are at.
❖ May he bless your going out and your coming in.
❖ May he lift you up.
❖ May you never be ashamed.
❖ And may your enemies never triumph over you.

# CHAPTER FOURTEEN

- ❖ Ooh God my father bless my day.
- ❖ Make me to know peace in this day.
- ❖ May the one who sits on the high chair help me.
- ❖ Let the right door be opened today.
- ❖ Wipe away my tear.
- ❖ Help me to overcome fear.
- ❖ Let this day be the beginning of good things in my life.
- ❖ Cause me to make it today.
- ❖ Do not let my enemies laugh at me.
- ❖ Do not let them say where is your God.
- ❖ Lord do not be silent in my life.
- ❖ Frustrate the plans of those who do wrong to me.
- ❖ Cause me to hold my head up high.
- ❖ Pour out a unique anointing over my life.
- ❖ Let me hear your voice.
- ❖ Teach me how to be a good worshiper.
- ❖ Put a love for the word in me.
- ❖ Above all oh God my father, keep me always on my knees before you.
- ❖ Keep me humble.
- ❖ You are my life.
- ❖ You are my hope.
- ❖ Do something good in my life.
- ❖ Stretch forth your hand and save me.
- ❖ Let your fingers rewrite my story.
- ❖ Let my life take off into bigger and better things.
- ❖ Help me to find my way.
- ❖ I ask for your guidance.
- ❖ Help me to condition my mind for success.

- ❖ Lord take care of me today.
- ❖ Show me how to keep on holding on.
- ❖ Let me be connected to the right people
- ❖ Order my steps from now on.
- ❖ Connect my spirit to your Holy Spirit.
- ❖ Open my eyes to see you.
- ❖ Open my mind to understand your word
- ❖ Open my ears to hear your voice.
- ❖ Open my mouth to tell others of you.

LIFE MAY SOMETIME PUSH YOU BEYOUND LIMIT.WHEN ALL HOPE SEEMS TO BE GONE, DRAW STRENGTH FROM EVERY PROMISE THAT GOD HAS PROMISE YOU. BE IT FROM THE WORD, DREAMS OR VISIONS OR PROPHESY. WHEN DAVID FELT DEPRESSED AND DEFEATED HE TOO HAD TO RELY ON GODS PROMISES.